CLAIRE WILKINS

(25)

Divorce Me, Darling!

A Musical Play

Sandy Wilson

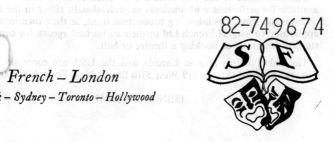

Samuel French – London
New York – Sydney – Toronto – Hollywood

CHARACTERS

Dulcie Dubois
Nancy Lebrun
Pierre Lebrun
Fay de la Falaise
Marcel de la Falaise
Alphonse Dubois
Maisie van Husen
Bobby van Husen
Polly Brockhurst
The Hon. Tony Brockhurst
Lord Brockhurst
Lady Brockhurst
Percival Browne (alias Mr Jones)
Mme Dubonnet (Mrs Percival Browne, alias Madame K)
Hortense, receptionist at the *Hotel du Paradis*
M. Gaston, manager of the *Hotel du Paradis*
Bell-boy
Girl in distress
Gendarme
The President of Monomania
Cecelia Doublewick ⎫
Prunella Oglethorpe ⎬ Health and Beauty Girls
Felicity Bagworth ⎭
Sir Freddy ffotherington-ffitch
Solange, a maid
Raoul, a waiter
Hannah van Husen
Manager of the *Café Pataplon*
Three American Sailors
Hotel Guests and **Staff, Holidaymakers** and **Diners** at the
   Café Pataplon

The action takes place in Nice

Divorce Me, Darling! was first produced at the Players Theatre in London on 9th December, 1964, and subsequently transferred to the Globe Theatre on 1st February, 1965. The first production of this revised version was given by the Tavistock Repertory Company at the Tower Theatre, London N.1 on 23rd March 1979, and was directed by Noël Howard.

MUSICAL NUMBERS

1	**Overture**	Orchestra
2	**Prologue**	Orchestra

ACT I

3	**Here We Are In Nice Again**	Dulcie, Nancy, Fay, Hortense and Ensemble
4	**Whatever Happened To Love?**	Polly, Dulcie, Nancy, Fay
5	**Someone To Dance With**	Bobby and Ensemble
5A	Melos for Bobby's exit	Orchestra
6	**Lights! Music!**	Mme Dubonnet and Ensemble
6A	Reprise: **Lights! Music!**	Mme Dubonnet, Hortense and Ensemble
7	**Maisie**	Marcel, Pierre, Alphonse
8	**Back To Nature**	Lady Brockhurst, Sir Freddy, Cecelia, Prunella, Felicity
8A	Reprise: **Back To Nature**	Orchestra
9	**On The Loose**	Lord Brockhurst, Dulcie, Nancy, Fay
10	**Monomanian National Anthem**	Orchestra
11	Melos: **Paradise Hotel**	Orchestra
11A	**Paradise Hotel**	Hortense, Gaston, Hotel Staff
12	Reprise: **Whatever Happened To Love?**	Orchestra
13	**No Harm Done**	Bobby, Polly
14	Interlude: **Paradise Hotel**	Orchestra
15	**Together Again**	Tony, Polly, Maisie, Bobby
16	Finaletto: **Paradise Hotel**	Hortense, Gaston, Hotel Staff
17	Entr'acte	Orchestra

ACT II

17A	Melos	Piano
18	**Divorce Me, Darling!**	Polly, Bobby, Tony, Maisie, Dulcie, Alphonse, Fay, Marcel, Nancy, Pierre
19	**Anthem**	Orchestra

No. 1 OVERTURE

No. 2 PROLOGUE

The Curtain *rises to reveal the Principals en tableau, in front of the tabs, in the following order: Hortense, Alphonse, Fay, Marcel, Lady Brockhurst, Lord Brockhurst, Percy, Mme Dubonnet, Dulcie, Tony, Polly, Bobby, Maisie, Nancy, Pierre*

The music coniinues softly, as Dulcie steps forward and addresses the Audience

Dulcie Oh—hello, everybody! I'm Dulcie. Remember? "Boop-a-doop, boop-a-doop" and all that . . .? Yes, that's me—or rather that *was* me—ten years ago, in nineteen-twenty-six, the year I got married. The year we *all* got married, as a matter of fact! Nancy married Pierre——

Nancy and Pierre come forward and bow and exit L

—Fay married Marcel——

Fay and Marcel do the same and exit L

—and I married—Alphonse . . .

Alphonse comer forward, attempts to join Dulcie, but she waves him away without looking at him. He shrugs resignedly, and exits L

Then there was Maisie—Mad-cap Maisie, as we used to call her. She did awfully well. She married a rich American—Bobbie van Husen!

Maisie and Bobby dance forward, curtsy and bow to the Audience and exit L

And Polly—well, of course, Polly did better than all of us. She married the Honourable Tony Brockhurst . . .

Polly and Tony dance forward, and exit L

Tony was the son of Lord and Lady Brockhurst . . .

Lord and Lady Brockhurst come forward and bow. Lord Brockhurst gives a little wave to Dulcei, who responds coyly. Lady Brockhurst, about to leave, notices

Lady Brockhurst Hubert!

He turns and follows her off R *sheepishly*

Dulcie Polly's father was a widower, and a millionaire—at least he used to be . . .

Percy comes forward and bows

How did it all happen? Well, it started at a finishing-school, in Nice, called the Villa Caprice. The headmistress was Madame Dubonnet——

Mme Dubonnet comes forward and bows

—and *she* got married too. To Polly's father!

Mme Dubonnet moves off, turns back to Percy, holding out her hand

Percy (*fervently*) Kiki!

He clasps her hand, and they exit L

Dulcie And that was more or less that . . .
Hortense Mam'selle Dulcie!
Dulcie What? (*Turning to her*) Oh heavens, I nearly forgot! This is Hortense—the *maid*. She kept us all in order—or tried to!

Hortense shakes her finger at Dulcie and exits L

But that was all ten years ago. Now it's nineteen-thirty-six and—(*looking at her watch*)—ye gods, I must rush or I'll miss the train. Toodle-oo!

She dashes off L *as the tabs part to reveal the full stage*

ACT I

Scene 1

The Foyer of the Hotel du Paradis. Morning

There are revolving doors UC which lead on to the promenade. UL is the entrance to the cocktail bar and UR a staircase which leads to the first floor. Next to the staircase is the reception desk

As the scene opens Hortense is standing behind the reception desk. The telephone rings and she answers it, telling the caller in mime that the hotel is full

At the same time M. Gaston enters C in a state

The Bell-boy enters L and M. Gaston shoos him out C

Hortense attempts to calm M. Gaston

The Bell-boy enters C carrying a load of suitcases and the Guests follow him in

No. 3 HERE WE ARE IN NICE AGAIN

Guests Here we are in Nice again
As we were last year
It's so jolly to
Have a holiday
Where the sea is so near.
Here on the French Riviera,
Haunt of Beauty and Rank,
Though each year it gets dearer,
It's still worth ev'ry franc.
That's why we're in Nice again
Where the sun shines bright.
Here we'll gaily
Get browner daily,
And then get blotto by night.
Others go to the
Island of Capri
Or the Isles of Greece.
We prefer to come back to ~~Nice~~ Nice!

As the song ends, Dulcie, Nancy and Fay enter C. They carry small suitcases

Fay Oh what bliss—there's a cocktail bar!

Hortense Mam'selle Fay!

Nancy Thank heavens we've arrived! Where are we?

Hortense Mam'selle Nancy!

Dulcie If I havn't got a room facing the sea, I'm going straight to *The Negresco*!

Hortense Mam'selle Dulcie!

Dulcie Look, girls—it's Hortense!

Nancy Hortense? Hortense who?

Dulcie Hortense, the *maid*—at the Villa Caprice . . .

All Where we were finished!

(*Singing*)   Here we are in Nice again
                After all these years.

Dulcie   I'm quite dizzy
               With joy. Oh, isn't it
               Simply heaven, my dears?

Nancy ⎫
Fay   ⎬   Here where we played the fool, girls,
               Larking down on the shore.

Hortense You were innocent school-girls!

Dulcie ⎫
Nancy ⎬   Well, we're not any more.
Fay   ⎭   That's why we're in Nice again
               In our youthful haunt.
               Don't misunderstand,
               Nothing underhand,
               Just a jolly old jaunt.
               It is utter bliss
               To experience this
               Feeling of release.
               We're so glad to come back to,
               Frightf'lly glad to come back to,
               Madly glad to come back to
               Nice!

Hortense But—where are your husbands?

Dulcie Our *husbands*? Oh, we left them behind—didn't we, girls?

Fay I'll say we did!

Dulcie, Nancy and Fay giggle

Hortense (*shaking her finger*) *Zut, alors!*

Dulcie But—can you keep a secret, Hortense?

Hortense nods eagerly

    We told *them* we were going to England, to see the Old Folks at Home.

Hortense *Mais—pourquoi?*

Fay They'd never have let us come back to Nice on our own. You know what French husbands are like.

Hortense *Hélas*—not yet!

Dulcie They're like french windows—lead you up the garden path.

Hortense *Mais non—absolument non!*

Dulcie *Mais oui*—utterly *oui*! So we've decided to turn the tables on them, and have a bang-up hol on our own . . .!
All That's why we're in Nice again
In our youthful haunt.
Don't misunderstand,
Nothing underhand,
Just a jolly old jaunt.
It is utter bliss.
To experience this
Feeling of release.
Tutti We're so glad to come back to,
Frightf'lly glad to come back to,
Madly glad to come back to
Nice!

The Guests exit

The music continues softly as Hortense introduces Dulcie, Nancy and Fay to Gaston who ushers them upstairs R

They exit chattering excitedly leaving Hortense alone

After a moment the Bell-boy enters carrying two monogrammed cases and a hat-box

Hortense *Qui est arrivé?*
Bell-boy Ze 'Onourable Missis Brockhurst!
Hortense Madame Polly Brockhurst?
Bell-boy *Oui—c'est elle!*

Hortense claps her hands in delight as the music swells and Polly enters C

During the following scene the Bell-boy takes the luggage upstairs

Polly Hortense! Here I am at last!
Hortense Oh, *chère madame*, it is so good to see you again.

They kiss

And you look so well!
Polly Thank you, Hortense. But I do feel a bit fagged from the Blue Train . . .
Hortense Then you must go to your suite—*toute de suite!* But—where is your husband—the Honourable Tony?
Polly Oh, he—he chucked at the last minute. He's so busy with the wretched estate. So I decided to come on my own.
Hortense But does he not need *les vacances* too?
Polly Oh yes, Hortense, he does! But sometimes I feel the old ancestral acres mean more to him than anything—even me . . .
Hortense Ah, *non. C'est impossible!*
Polly We used to say we'd be happy with just a room in—well, Kensington or even Bloomsbury. But of course we were younger then . . .

Sounds of laughter off L

Hortense And soon you will be feeling young again! *Regardez, madame . . .!*

Dulcie, Nancy and Fay, wearing beach pyjamas and wide-brimmed hats, enter R

Polly (*turning*) What . . .?
Dulcie (*seeing Polly, and stopping dead in her tracks*) Look, girls! It's Polly!
Nancy Polly . . .? Oh, *Polly!*

They all greet each other effusively, much to Hortense's delight

Fay But—where's Tony?
Polly I was telling Hortense: he's too busy to take a hol.
Dulcie
Nancy }(*together*){ Just like our husbands!
Fay
Polly Really?
Dulcie Yes—dreary beasts!
Polly (*sadly*) Sometimes I wonder why we were all so keen to get married . . .

No. 4   WHATEVER HAPPENED TO LOVE?

(*Singing*)   When we were younger
                We used to hunger
                For that certain thing we called a Boy Friend.

Dulcie
Nancy }   Boy Friend!
Fay

Polly   And then we found him,
                And we could hardly wait
                To build our lives around him
                And to become his mate.

Nancy   Love was ours,
                And it was all we needed.

Fay   Like spring flowers
                We blossomed in the sun.

Dulcie   But time went by,
                And as our youth receded,

All   The joys that once we knew
                Began to fade from view.

Polly   And now I sometimes sit and sadly wonder
                Where did romance disappear to?
                And why did it vanish away?
                And how can the one I was dear to
                And was so very near to
                Seem a stranger today?
                When April still comes around ev'ry year too,
                And stars go on shining above,

	When ev'ry song-bird upon the wing
	Still has a song to sing,
	Then tell me
	Whatever happened to love?
Dulcie ⎫	
Nancy ⎬	We often ask the same question:
Fay ⎭	
Polly	Where
Dulcie ⎫	
Nancy ⎬	Won't you please tell me where
Fay ⎭	
Polly	Did romance disappear to?
	And why
Dulcie ⎫	
Nancy ⎬	Won't you please tell me why
Fay ⎭	
Polly	Did it vanish away?
Dulcie ⎫	
Nancy ⎬	So far away
Fay ⎭	
Polly	And how
Dulcie ⎫	
Nancy ⎬	I just want to know how
Fay ⎭	
Polly	Can the one I was dear to
	And was so very near to
	Seem a stranger today?
Dulcie ⎫	
Nancy ⎬	It's all so strange
Fay ⎭	
Polly	When April still
Dulcie ⎫	
Nancy ⎬	Ev'ry spring April still
Fay ⎭	
Polly	Comes around ev'ry year too,
	And stars
Dulcie ⎫	
Nancy ⎬	All those thousands of stars
Fay ⎭	
Polly	Go on shining above
Dulcie ⎫	
Nancy ⎬	So high above
Fay ⎭	
Polly	When ev'ry song-bird upon the wing
	Still has a song to sing
	Then tell me whatever happened
All	Whatever happened
Polly	Whatever happened to love?

Dulcie ⎫
Nancy ⎬   Whatever happened to love?
Fay   ⎭

Hortense But you must not be so sad! The season is just beginning! And tomorrow night there is a Gala re-opening of the *Café Pataplon*.

Dulcie The *Café Pataplon*—where we were proposed to!

Fay The night of the Carnival Ball!

Nancy Did I go too?

The others laugh

Hortense There will be *un Grand Cabaret* with an International Star . . . !

Polly Oh, who?

Nancy Florence Desmond?

Fay Hildegarde?

Dulcie Douglas Byng?

Hortense No—someone quite new to Nice. She is staying here at the *Hotel du Paradis*, but no-one, not even I, knows her real name. She is called—Madame K!

All Madame K!

Dulcie How madly intriguing!

Hortense And they say that the Gala will be attended by the President of Monomania.

Nancy Monomania? Isn't that a new dance?

Dulcie Oh, you are a chump, Nancy. It's a country—in South America.

Fay Where all the platinum comes from. When's he arriving, Hortense?

Hortense He is here already. His yacht is in the harbour!

Dulcie What a thrill! I say, girls let's all go and have a squizz!

Fay Righto! Are you coming, Polly?

Polly No, I think I'd like to see my room.

Hortense But of course, madame.

Dulcie See you later then . . .

They exit C, *chattering excitedly, as Hortense ushers Polly upstairs* R

A girl runs out of the cocktail bar L *in a state of distress as Gaston enters* R

Girl Really! I've never been so insulted!

Gaston What is the matter, madame?

Girl That man in there, that drunken American—he tried to—to *molest* me!

Gaston (*horror-struck*) *Mon dieu*, it is not possible, here in the *Hotel du Paradis*!

Gaston exits L

Bobby appears L, *walking jauntily and a little tipsily*

During the following scene the Guests drift on and Hortense enters from upstairs R

Girl That's him!

No. 5 SOMEONE TO DANCE WITH

Bobby   Lady, oh Lady,
             Please don't be distressed.
             Lady, there's nothing shady
             About my behaviour.
             That look I gave yer
             Was only meant to convey a simple request,
             Please believe me.

             Don't be afraid,
             I'm no gay young blade
             Out to make the grade.
             I'm just looking round
             For someone to dance with.

             Make no mistake,
             I am not a rake
             Who is on the make.
             I'm just looking round
             For someone to dance with.

             If you're keen on waltzing,
             I'd be glad to waltz.
             If you'd rather fox-trot,
             I'll give that fox-trot ev'rything I've got.

             So please relent
             And you'll make this gent
             Blissfully content
             Just to know he's found
             That someone to dance with.

The chorus is repeated musically, and Bobby dances with the Lady Guests

Bobby   If you'd care to tango,
             I can tango too.
             If you'd rather rhumba,
             I'll do the rhumba times without number.

Bobby   I'm not a cad,   **Guests** He's not a cad,
             I'm a simple lad   He's a simple lad

Bobby and Who'd be very glad
Guests   Just to know that you
             Are somebody who
             Will condescend to
             Be someone to dance with.

At the end of the number the Guests exit

Bobby is about to exit L, *when Polly enters down the stairs* R, *and he sees her*

Bobby Well, I'll be . . .!

Polly sees him, but does not recognize him

It is—Polly, isn't it?

Polly Yes, but I don't think I . . . Good Lord, it's Bobby—Bobby van Husen!

They great each other warmly

How's Maisie?

Bobby Oh, she's fine—I guess . . .

Polly Don't you *know*?

Bobby Well, you see, Polly, it's like this. I'm here, in Nice . . .

Polly Yes?

Bobby But Maisie's there—(*pointing vaguely*)—in London. With my sister, Hannah. My *older* sister.

Polly (*puzzled*) Oh? But why aren't you in London too?

Bobby Well—Hannah's husband-hunting, and Maisie's rounding up the game. Hannah wanted a Dook, but it seems the Dooks are all spoken for. Last time I saw her she was willing to settle for an Oil. I didn't want to stick around until she'd worked her way down to the plain Esks.

Polly Esks?

Bobby You know how the English write, when they mean Mister So-and-so So-and-so Esq?

Polly Oh, I see! So—you came down here?

Bobby That's right . . . (*Noticing Polly's expression*) Say, are you on your own too?

Polly nods

Then—why don't we have dinner together?

Polly That's very sweet of you, Bobby but—I don't know if I should . . .

Bobby Oh hell, why not? We've known each other for ten years!

Polly (*brightening*) Yes, we have, haven't we?

Bobby Cocktails in the bar at seven-thirty—and wear your glad rags!

Cue No. 5A. *Music*

Bobby dances off L, *waving goodbye to Polly who waves back*

Polly begins to exit C *as Mme Dubonnet enters downstairs* R. *She starts on seeing Polly and draws a veil across her face*

When Polly has gone, Mme Dubonnet goes quickly to reception and rings the bell

Hortense enters behind the desk R

Hortense Madame K! You rang?

Mme Dubonnet Tell me please—who was that lady in grey? Was it the Honourable Madame Tony Brockhurst?

Hortense (*surprised*) Why yes, madame! You know her?

Mme Dubonnet (*ironically*) *Know* her? She is my—(*lowering her voice*)— Hortense . . .

Hortense Madame knows my name?

Mme Dubonnet Yes—I do. Hortense, can I trust you?

Hortense I—I think so, madame.

Mme Dubonnet (*with a laugh*) But of course I can—I should remember that!

Hortense Remember . . .?

Mme Dubonnet Yes—remember! (*She throws aside her veil*)

Hortense *Mais non! Ce n'est pas possible!* You are . . .

Mme Dubonnet Yes, Hortense. I—am Madame Dubonnet! Or rather I *was* . . .

Hortense But you are Madame Percival Browne—Mrs Brockhurst's step-mother! She will be so pleased to see you . . .

Mme Dubonnet No, Hortense! She must not know I am here . . .

Hortense is about to interject

C'est une histoire longue—a long story. But to be brief, my husband—Monsieur Browne—lost all his money in the Crash. Then he was accused of selling shares in a non-existent platinum mine . . .

Hortense *Mon Dieu!*

Mme Dubonnet He was forced to flee to South America, and I—I became a Cabaret Star. But I did not wish little Polly to be ashamed of me, so I also became a blonde and changed my name.

Hortense To Madame K!

Mme Dubonnet K—for Kiki. That is what he used to call me. So now you understand, Hortense, why I do not wish her to see me—although I long to see *her*, to know that she is happy.

Hortense (*uncertainly*) I—I think she is, madame.

Mme Dubonnet Ah, Hortense, I hope so. The world today is rather *triste* . . .

Hortense *Vraiment, madame?*

No. 6 LIGHTS! MUSIC!

Mme Dubonnet   Oh yes, Hortense, and you are very lucky
To be as calm and happy as you are,
For you have no idea how very plucky
You have to be when you become a star.
If you believe it's just a life of glamour,
Of jewels and furs and parties all night long,
Of critics' praise and fans' adoring clamour,
Believe me, *chère* Hortense, you would be wrong.
Behind the Theatre's glittering façade
There lurks a world that's cruel, cold and hard
And night after night you have got to go on,
Though your heart may be wracked with despair.
You may hate it and yet
You must never forget
That the audience is waiting—out there!
So it's

Lights! Music! And on with the show!
Remember you're playing a *rôle*.
Light! Music! And no-one must know
The depths of that ache in your soul.
On with the grease-paint to hide the strain of it,
Make up your face with a smile.
Once you're a star, you don't dare complain of it,
Bear the pain of it
For a while,
And give them
Tears, laughter, and earn your applause,
And then, when the curtain descends,
What comes after the public ignores,
And God only knows how it ends.
You long to scream your career is weighing you
Down and laying you
Low. No!
Up off your knees,
For the Theatre decrees
It's Lights! Music! And on with the show.

The Guests drift on L and R as Mme Dubonnet sings. The song is repeated

All
Lights! Music! And on with the show!
Remember you're playing a *rôle*.
Lights! Music! And no-one must know
The depths of that ache in your soul.
On with the grease-paint to hide the strain of it,
Make up your face with a smile.
If you're a star, you don't dare complain of it,
Bear the pain of it
For a while,
And give them
Tears, laughter, and earn your applause,
And then, when the curtain descends,
What comes after the public ignores,
And God only knows how it ends.
You long to scream your career is weighing you
Down and laying you
Low. No!
Up off your knees,
For the Theatre decrees
It's lights! Music!
Lights! Music!
Lights! Music!
And on with the show!

*After the applause the music continues. There is the sound of cheering off
stage*

The Bell-boy runs on C

Bell-boy The President is coming ashore!

The Guests react excitedly

Mme Dubonnet The President—the President of where, Hortense?
Hortense Monomania, madame. In South America.
Mme Dubonnet (*reacting*) South America . . .! (*She clutches Hortense's arm*) Remember, Hortense! Not a word! Just . . .

No. 6A   LIGHTS! MUSIC! (*Reprise*)

(*Singing*)   Lights! Music!

Hortense   Lights! Music!
All   Lights! Music! And on with the show!

The Guests move downstage, cheering the President, as the front cloth comes in

SCENE 2

The Promenade des Anglais. A moment later

The front cloth depicts the Promenade des Anglais with an advertising kiosk L *showing a poster announcing the Gala re-opening of the "Café Pataplon" and featuring a portrait of Madame K*

The cheering continues, and Dulcie, Nancy and Fay enter L *and join in*

A Gendarme enters R, *making way for the President who follows behind him. The President is a resplendent figure in a heavily be-medalled uniform, wearing dark glasses and smoking a cigar. He crosses, waving and saluting and follows the Gendarme off* L. *Everyone exits* L, *cheering and chattering*

Marcel enters R

Marcel Pierre! Pierre! Where are you?

Pierre enters L

Pierre Here I am, Marcel. Where is Alphonse?

Alphonse enters backwards L

Alphonse Pierre! Marcel! Where are you?
Marcel ⎫
Pierre ⎭ (*together*) ⎰ Here we are, Alphonse!
Alphonse (*turning*) Oh, thank goodness! I thought I had lost you.
Marcel From now on we must stick together, *hein*?
Pierre *Certainement!*

They all clasp hands

Oh, does it not feel good to be back in Nice again?
Marcel *Mais oui!* And to be bachelors again!
Alphonse (*shocked*) Bachelors! *Ah non*, Marcel. I still love my wife . . .

Pierre *Bien sur!* And so do I—*chère* Nancy!

Marcel *Chère* Fay!

Alphonse *Chère* Dulcie . . . (*Suddenly panicking*) I must go 'ome!

Pierre
Marcel } (*grabbing him*) *Non*, Alphonse! { (*Together*)

Pierre We haven't even been *sur la plage!*

Alphonse *La plage?*

Marcel *Oui* . . . ! (*He makes swimming gestures*)

Alphonse *Ah, non!*

Marcel Oh, Alphonse, 'ow you have changed!

Alphonse Me? *Changé?*

Marcel Yes indeed, *mon ami* . . .

No. 7   MAISIE

(*Singing*)   Ten years ago when we were single,
We weren't so bashful and discreet.
We never missed a chance to mingle
With ev'ry demoiselle we'd meet.

Pierre   All of them young and pretty;
Most of them I forget.
But there was just one
Who was so much fun
I can see her even yet.

All   Ev'ry now and then in Spring
I find my thoughts are wandering
To Maisie,
She was so crazy
But oh, so sweet.

When I feel a summer breeze
It seems to carry memories
Of Maisie.
No cloud that floats in the sky was freer
And even now I seem to see her

Twinkling just like star-dust,
Sparkling like champagne.
I would travel far just
To see her again.

And often to myself I say,
When Autumn turns the skies to grey,
And leaves begin to tumble from the bough,
I wonder where Maisie is now?

The refrain is repeated with a dance routine

Ev'ry now and then in Spring
I find my thoughts are wandering
To Maisie,

She was so crazy
But oh, so sweet.

When I feel a summer breeze
It seems to carry memories
Of Maisie.
No cloud that floats in the sky was freer
And even now I seem to see her

Twinkling just like star-dust,
Sparkling like champagne.
I would travel far just
To see her again.

And often to myself I say,
When Autumn turns the skies to grey,
And leaves begin to tumble from the bough,
I wonder where Maisie—
That crazy, sweet Maisie—
I wonder where Maisie is now?

There is the sound of singing off stage as Lady Brockhurst, Cecelia, Felicity, Prunella and Sir Freddy sing the first six lines of "Back To Nature"

The Gendarme enters R, *looking apprehensive*

Marcel *Qu'est ce que c'est, monsieur?*
Gendarme *C'est les* Brockhursts!
Alphonse
Marcel   } *(together)* { *Les* Brockhursts! *Nom d'un nom!*
Pierre

Alphonse, Marcel, Pierre and the Gendarme exit hurriedly L *as Lady Brockhurst enters* R, *followed by Cecelia, Felicity, Prunella and Sir Freddy. They are all dressed in hiking costume and carry placards extolling* HEALTH AND BEAUTY

No. 8 BACK TO NATURE

All Back to Nature, that's the cry,
It's a cry you would be foolish to deny.
Why not leave the grim Metropolis
And start to stride,
For the place to make you top-whole is
The country-side.
Back to Nature, join the band,
Once you're under canvas life is simply grand.
And wherever you are and whatever you do,
Mother Nature's calling you.

She's calling you in Liverpool,
In London and in Leeds,
She's singing out her golden rule

To anyone who heeds:
Forget the City's scurry
With its worry and its care
Strap your rucksack on and hurry
To the open air.

Back to Nature, come away!
What is there to stop you joining us today?
You'll have no more coughs and sneezes
Playing outdoor sports,
And it's grand to feel the breezes
Blowing up your shorts.
Back to Nature! Can't you hear?
It's a summons that is ringing loud and clear.
You must never deny her, whatever you do,
Mother Nature's calling you!

Lady Brockhurst Squadron—halt! Stand at ease! I will now call the roll.
Felicity Bagworth!
Felicity Here, ma'am!
Lady Brockhurst Prunella Oglethorpe!
Prunella Here, ma'am!
Lady Brockhurst Cecelia Doublewick!
Cecelia Here, ma'am!
Lady Brockhurst Sir Frederick ffotherington-ffitch!
Sir Freddy Herew I am, Aunty—I mean, ma'am!
Lady Brockhurst (*with a withering look*) Lord Hubert Brockhurst!

There is no reply. The troop look nervous

Lord Hubert Brockhurst!

There is still no reply

Am I to understand we have a deserter in our midst?
Sir Freddy Oh, Aunt Hilda, that's a tewwible thing to say!
Lady Brockhurst Where is he then? (*In stentorian tones*) Hubert!

Lord Brockhurst enters R *wearing plus-fours and carrying a placard which
reads:* NEVER TOO LATE TO BE HEALTHY

Lord Brockhurst Here, m'dear. I was just admiring the view.
Lady Brockhurst Fiddlesticks! I noticed you going out of step several
miles ago, *and* I know the reason why. Kindly join the ranks.

*Lord Brockhurst stands next to Cecelia, nudging her. She giggles and Lady
Brockhurst blows a whistle*

Stand easy! Well, fellow health-seekers, we are now on the second lap
of our pilgrimage. Having infiltrated Paris——
Lord Brockhurst (*sotto voce*) And how!
Lady Brockhurst—we are about to convert the Côte d'Azur. Tomorrow
night we shall have an excellent opportunity. There is to be a Gala

re-opening of the *Café Pataplon*—(*indicating the poster*)—and we shall attend——

Lord Brockhurst looks delighted and nudges Sir Freddy

—in order to give a display of Swedish Drill and Physical Jerks.

Lord Brockhurst's face falls

In the meanwhile we have to find a suitable place to pitch camp. I propose that we should split up, in order to reconnoitre every possibility, and reassemble here at two hours from now precisely. Any questions?

Sir Freddy Please, Aunt Hilda, I—I don't speak any Fwench.

Lady Brockhurst That is of no consequence. When in doubt, use sign language.

Lord Brockhurst (*sotto voce*) I know one sign in particular . . .

Cue No. 8A. *Music*

Lady Brockhurst (*blowing her whistle*) Squadron—dismiss! Left, right, left, right . . .

Lady Brockhurst, Felicity, and Prunella march off L *in time to the music while Lord Brockhurst, Sir Freddy and Cecelia march off* R. *A pretty girl enters* R *and Lord Brockhurst enters following her with Sir Freddy following him*

Sir Freddy I say—Uncle Hubert!

Lord Brockhurst Go away, Freddy! Go away!

Sir Freddy But—but oughtn't we to stick together?

Lord Brockhurst You stick together with Cecelia. I've got a little unfinished business to attend to in Nice.

Sir Freddy But what will Aunt Hilda say?

Lord Brockhurst (*taking Sir Freddy's arm*) Listen, my boy, how old are you?

Sir Freddy Thirty-thwee and a half

Lord Brockhurst Thirty-three and a half . . .? And have you ever been in the South of France before?

Sir Freddy shakes his head

Then go and "reconnoitre every possibility"—like me!

He swivels Sir Freddy around and pushes him off R

Rubbing his hands Lord Brockhurst prepares to follow the girl who went off L *as Dulcie enters* R *with Nancy and Fay following a little way behind*

Dulcie (*turning to Nancy and Fay*) There you are, you two! I was positive it was him. (*Turning back and waving*) Coo-ee! Lord Brockhurst!

Lord Brockhurst turns reluctantly

Lord Brockhurst (*recognizing them*) Well I'm blowed! The three little maids from school!

Dulcie Yes! Only we're not so little now!

Lord Brockhurst (*chucking her under the chin*) And what, may I ask, are you doing in Nice?

Dulcie Wouldn't you like to know?

The girls giggle

Fay And what about you, Lord Brockhurst? Are you here on a rest cure?

Lord Brockhurst Well, I know what'll cure me—and it isn't a rest!

They all laugh immoderately

Dulcie Oh, you are the dreaded end!

Lord Brockhurst But seriously, my dears—you won't split on me, will you?

Dulcie Not if you promise not to split on us!

Lord Brockhurst (*shaking her hand*) Done!

No. 9   ON THE LOOSE

Dulcie ⎫ **Nancy** ⎬ **Fay** ⎭	You can rely on us
Lord Brockhurst **All**	You can rely on me For we are pals together, Just as we used to be.
Dulcie ⎫ **Nancy** ⎬ **Fay** ⎭	We'll never make a fuss When you are on the spree.
Lord Brockhurst	For a little freedom now and then Is essential to the best of men.
Dulcie	And to the best of girls as well, Don't you agree?
Lord Brockhurst	Oh yes, I do Agree with you.
	Just once in a while It's nice to be on the loose, On the loose and fancy-free.
	Just once in a while To slip from the marriage noose Can almost make me seem to be again
	An age I'll never see again. I may be old, But if a girl finds me attractive, I feel consoled For being almost totally inactive.
	Just once in a while It's terribly nice to be On the loose and fancy-free.
Dulcie	Just once in a while

It's nice to be on the loose,
On the loose and fancy-free.

Just once in a while
To slip from the marriage noose
And go and join the social whirl again
Can make me feel a girl again.

Fay   I'd never let
Dulcie   A man who's not my husband pat me,
Nancy   But I still get
All   A little thrill when someone whistles at me.

Just once in a while
It's terribly nice to be
On the loose and fancy-free.

The chorus is repeated with "jazz-band" effects: Lord Brockhurst representing a double bass, and the girls playing other instruments in mime

After the applause, all exit L

Percy enters R, *in a tropical suit and wearing dark glasses. He glances at the poster, and is about to look more closely, when the Gendarme enters* L, *ushering on the President*

Gendarme *Voilà, Monsieur le Président.* I think we have escaped the crowds.

President *Muchas gracias,* officer.

The Gendarme salutes and exits L

The President looks around suspiciously, as does Percy. Finding the coast clear, they move swiftly together and shake hands

Percy Señor President!

President *Querido amigo!* You have kept our rendezvous!

Percy Of course.

President You have served me faithfully, Señor Jones, and I shall miss you. Your mind—she is made up?

Percy Yes. I am determined to face my accusers and clear my name.

President Your name? Tell me, *mi amigo*, it is not—Jones, is it?

Percy looks away

Well, no matter, I must not be so *curioso.* But may I make one more request of you?

Percy By all means.

President Tomorrow night I am due to appear at a Gala, but for reasons which I cannot reveal, even to you, I must be elsewhere. Now, *mi amigo*, will you go in my place?

Percy I, señor?

President *Si.* We are nearly the same build. With the aid of a false beard and one of my uniforms, you could pass easily for *el Presidente de* Monomania.

Percy I am at your command.

The Gendarme enters L

Gendarme *Pardon, Monsieur le Président,* but you are awaited by *Monsieur le Maire.*

Cue No. 10. *The Monomanian National Anthem strikes up in the distance*

President (*with a shrug*) Oh well—back to work!

Percy salutes. The President returns his salute and, is about to go

President Oh, Señor Jones . . .
Percy Yes, señor?
President The Gala—she is at the *Café Pataplon.*

He exits L, *followed by the Gendarme*

Percy The *Café Pataplon?* (*He turns to the poster, takes off his dark-glasses and reads it more closely. Then reeling back, with a gasp*) Kiki . . .!

The music comes up to full, as the Lights fade to Black-out

Cue No. 11. *Music*

SCENE 3

Two balconies in the Hotel du Paradis. That night

The front cloth goes up to reveal two adjoining balconies. There is a parapet which runs DC *separating the two balconies. This is later turned or revolved to become a piano. Two pairs of french windows* R *and* L *lead into two suites: the Brockhurst's* R *and the van Husen's* L. *The Brockhurst's has an exit* R *and the van Husen's* L, *and both suites are connected backstage* C. *Against the offstage wall of each is a console table with a mirror above it. On the table in the Brockhurst suite stands a framed photograph of Tony while on the table in the van Husen suite is a photograph of Maisie. On each balcony is a small wrought-iron table and chair. On the floor above* C *is a window with shutters*

As the Lights come up the music plays softly

Hortense enters the Brockhurst suite followed by Solange who carries a vase of flowers. Hortense indicates where the vase is to go, gives the flowers a final touch and dismisses Solange. Then she comes out on to the balcony and enjoys the view. Gaston enters the van Husen suite followed by Raoul who carries a tray on which there are two glasses and an ice-bucket containing a bottle of champagne. Gaston indicates where the tray is to go and dismisses Raoul. Gaston glances out on to the balcony to see that all is well and catches sight of Hortense

Gaston Mam'selle Hortense!
Hortense Monsieur Gaston! *Quelle surprise!*

Gaston (*joining her*) Not an unpleasant surprise, I trust!
Hortense *Non, non.* It is always a pleasure to see you.
Gaston (*with a bow*) Forgive me, mam'selle, but it is difficult for me to
remember that our relation is that of *employeur* and . . .
Hortense *Employée?*
Gaston *Exactement.* I would wish it to be more—more equal . . .
Hortense *Vraiment?*
Gaston More close . . .
Hortense *Oh là là!* Then you mean that we should be . . .
Gaston (*eagerly*) Yes, yes . . .
Hortense Partners?
Gaston (*slightly taken aback*) Partners? Of course, but perhaps not just
in business, but also . . .
Hortense There is no need to explain. I think I understand . . .

No. 11A   PARADISE HOTEL

(*Singing*)	Wouldn't it be
	Lovely if we
	Two could agree
	To team up
	I'm sure that we could dream up
	A future for us to share.

Gaston   *Mais, s'il vous plaît*
              Can I just say
              That I have drawn a scheme up
              By which we could combine
              To make this place of mine
              A grand hotel beyond compare.

Hortense   I think I know the kind
              Of place you have in mind:
              Twould be for folks who roam
              A home from home.

              All the guests will be so happy
              When they fall beneath its spell,
              And the smart and the discerning
              Ev'ry year will be returning
              To the Paradise Hotel.

              For the service will be snappy
              Ev'ry time you ring your bell
              So we know that you'll donate a
              Tip to ev'ry maid and waiter
              At the Paradise Hotel.

              Ah-ah, ooh-ooh,
              What wonderful things we'll do!
              Ooh-ooh, ah-ah,
              Life will be one long tra-la-la-la.

Gaston	In each bridal suite a chappy
Hortense	With his brand new bride will dwell,
	And there'll be a quite unknown suite
	That is going to be our own suite
	At the Paradise Hotel.

During the second chorus Solange, Raoul and other members of the staff appear on the balconies and at the window and join in

All   For a holiday so happy
                   That you'll bid your cares farewell
                   Ev'ry guide will recommend you,
                   Thomas Cook himself will send you
                   To the Paradise Hotel.

                   And our menu's far from scrappy,
                   For our chefs will all excel,
                   And you're going to read a fine list
                   When you ask to read the wine list
                   At the Paradise Hotel.

                   Heigh-ho, ho-hum,
                   What masses of guests will come!
                   Ho-hum, heigh-ho
                   And they'll never ever want to go.

Gaston	If a mother needs a nappy,
Hortense	We'll supply the cot as well,
	And perhaps before long we two
	Will require a nursery too
	At the Paradise Hotel.

Hortense, Gaston, Solange, Raoul and the staff exit

A moment later Polly enters the Brockhurst suite R. She wears white fox furs over a white satin evening dress, and is saying goodnight to Bobby

Polly Well—goodnight, Bobby, and thank you so much . . .
Bobby (*off*) Goodnight, Polly. Sleep tight!

Polly picks up the photograph of Tony, sighs, kisses it and replaces it. She comes out on to the balcony, removes her furs and lays them on the table

Bobby enters the van Husen suite. He is in tails, with top hat and white silk scarf

He chucks away his top hat, picks up the photograph of Maisie, winks at it, kisses it, shrugs and replaces it. He sees the champagne, rubs his hands and is about to open it, when a thought strikes him. He tiptoes out on to the balcony. Polly, who is deep in thought, does not see him

Bobby (*coughing*) Ahem!
Polly (*startled*) Oh—! Bobby! What—what are you doing there?
Bobby I—I'm afraid this is my terrace.

Polly (*embarrassed*) Oh . . .

Bobby Now, don't get the wrong idea. When I found out, I tried to have my room changed, but the hotel's full up. I guess Hortense thought you and Tony would *like* to be next door, as we're old friends.

Polly Oh, it doesn't matter. After all, it's perfectly true. We *are* old friends . . .

Bobby (*trying to laugh it off*) Sure! (*After a pause*) Some view!

Polly Yes . . .

Bobby You see that yacht—the big one?

Polly Yes.

Bobby It's——

Bobby }
Polly } (*together*) { —the President of Monomania's!

They laugh and the tension is broken

Bobby Say, as we *are* old friends, how about joining me in a night-cap?

Polly Oh, I don't think . . .

Bobby Nothing strong—just champagne. We could have it out here on the balcony and drink to—absent friends?

Polly Well—yes, I'd love to!

Bobby Swell!

Cue No. 12. *Music*

Bobby ushers Polly through to his balcony

Polly Oh, listen! The band is playing in the garden.

Bobby The French always did have perfect timing.

Bobby opens the champagne and pours two glasses

Bobby (*giving one to Polly*) *Voilà, madame!*

Polly *Merci, monsieur!*

Bobby To Tony!

Polly To Maisie!

They drink. Polly is suddenly stricken with remorse

Bobby What's wrong, Polly? Is the champagne flat?

Polly No, It's just that—I was wondering what they would think, if they could see us now.

Bobby What should they think? We're not doing anything wrong, are we?

Polly No—I suppose not.

Bobby Of course we aren't . . . (*He puts his glass down on the tray and goes to the parapet. He turns it round to reveal the piano and, sitting at it, mimes playing the accompaniment to the song*)

No. 13   NO HARM DONE

(*Singing*)   Don't you see, for heaven's sake,
You and I deserve a break
From the monotone of the marriage routine?

And there's not a thing amiss
In a rendezvous like this,
That is, just as long as we keep the party clean!
Here's a simple way of explaining what I mean:

There's no harm done
If we drink champagne.
Our reputations are free from stain.
Our conversation never offends,
And what's a glass of wine between friends?
There's no harm done
If I kiss your hand,
And say the evening has been just grand,
And if it ends the way it's begun,
Then tell me, what's the harm of it?
Surely that's the charm of it:
We've had fun,
But there's no harm done.

Polly You may be right, Bobby, but just the same I—I think I'd better say goodnight. I have had rather a long day, and—well, I do feel we're being a little—unwise . . .

She puts her glass down on the tray and moves away

Bobby   There's no harm done
                 If we drink champagne
Polly   Our reputations are free from stain . . .

Bobby touches her hand

(*Speaking*) Oh . . .!

They dance around the balcony

(*Striking a pose*) No, Bobby, we really shouldn't be behaving like this. You've been terribly sweet, and I've had a simply marvellous time, but I do think we should say goodnight now, before—before we do anything—silly . . .

She is about to go but Bobby resumes the song

Bobby   Our conversation never offends
Polly   And what's a glass of wine between friends?

They dance through both the suites and out on to the balcony again, in the course of which Bobby drops his scarf in the Brockhurst suite

Both   Then tell me, what's the harm of it?
                 Surely that's the charm of it:
                 We've had fun
                 But there's no harm done.

When the number ends, the telephone rings in the Brockhurst suite and Polly goes to answer it. Bobby turns the parapet round

Polly Hello? . . . Yes . . . Tony! Where are you? . . . Here? In Nice? . . .
Downstairs? (*She is rather shaken*) Oh! . . . Of course I'm glad you're
here, darling. I'm just so—so surprised. Shall I come down? . . . Oh,
you're coming up? . . . Yes, of course. I'll see you in a minute . . . (*She
rings off, and comes on to the balcony*) That was Tony. He's here, in the
hotel!

Bobby That's swell! When did he arrive?

Polly I—I don't know. Just now, I suppose. Oh dear, I don't know why,
but I feel a bit guilty . . .

Bobby Guilty? What about, Polly?

Polly Nothing—nothing at all . . . Well, I'd better—tidy up. Goodnight,
Bobby.

Bobby Goodnight, Polly, and say hello to Tony for me.

Polly Oh—yes. Yes, I will. And thank you again. It *was* a lovely evening.

*Polly returns to her suite. Bobby pauses a moment, shakes his head, and then
goes into his suite*

> *There is a knock on the door of the Brockhurst suite, and Tony enters* R,
> *wearing travelling clothes*

(*Rushing into his arms*) Tony! When did you arrive?

Tony Just a few minutes ago. I took the lunch-time plane from Croydon.

Polly What made you decide to come after all?

Tony (*stiffly*) Well, I'd been working dashed hard and I felt I needed a
break. That's all . . .

Polly Oh. Didn't you—miss me a little?

Tony Naturally. I mean to say—did *you* miss *me*?

Polly Oh terribly, darling! I was nearly coming straight home again.

Tony Were you? Well—(*with an awkward laugh*)—good thing you didn't,
isn't it?

Polly Yes . . . Oh, Tony, do come out and see the view. It's heavenly!

She leads him on to the balcony

Tony Whose is that yacht?

Polly The President of Monomania's

Tony (*disapprovingly*) It's bigger than the Duke of Westminster's.

Polly Oh, that reminds me! You're just in time for the Gala re-opening
of the *Café Pataplon*!

Tony The Café what?

Poly Oh, Tony, don't say you've forgotten!

Tony Forgotten what?

Polly The *Café Pataplon*. That's where—where we got engaged, the
night of the Carnival Ball.

Tony (*embracing her*) Oh yes, so it was. But that's a hell of a long time
ago, old girl.

Polly (*breaking away*) Yes. I suppose it is . . .

The telephone rings in the van Husen suite and Bobby answers it

Bobby Hullo? . . .

Tony (*noticing the scarf and picking it up*) I say, you've dropped something.

Polly Have I? (*Recognizing the scarf*) Oh, Tony, I meant to tell you . .

Bobby Maisie! Where are you? . . . (*He continues talking on the telephone during the following*)

Tony But this is a man's scarf . . .

Polly Yes. That's what I was going to . . .

Tony With the initial R on it. How did it get here?

Polly If you'd just let me explain . . .

Tony And why are you all dressed up like that?

Polly Because—(*changing her mind*)—why shouldn't I be? I'm on holiday, and this is a smart hotel.

Tony So I can see. With lots of smart customers. This is a very expensive scarf.

Polly Is it really? I hadn't noticed.

Tony Whose is it?

Polly I haven't the least idea.

Tony Are you sure?

Polly (*with an effort*) Positive.

Tony How does it happen to be here?

Polly I imagine someone dropped it.

Tony (*dubiously*) Yes—yes, I imagine so . . . Well, I think I shall have a bath. I hope they have good plumbing in this *smart* hotel! (*He stumps inside*)

Bobby has rung off and is pacing up and down in his suite. Polly crosses to his balcony

Polly (*calling softly*) Bobby!

Bobby (*coming out on to the balcony*) Polly! What's wrong?

Polly I've done the most terrible thing. Tony found your scarf, and I—I pretended I didn't know whose it was.

Bobby You *did?*

Polly Oh, Bobby, it sounds dreadful, but I wanted to make him jealous. Am I being wicked?

Bobby No, I think you're being smart. Say, I've got news too. Maisie's here!

Polly Oh, no!

Bobby Oh, yes!

There is a prolonged rapping on the door of the van Husen suite

That'll be her. We'll have a grand reunion tomorrow, won't we?

Polly nods emphatically, and they return to their respective suites

Maisie enters L at high speed, wearing a travelling suit and furs

Maisie Bobby! Bobby! Where are you? Oh, there you are! (*Offering her cheek to be kissed*) I'm utterly exhausted—travelling for hours in that *ghastly* foreign train, eating that *ghastly* foreign food, with all those *ghastly* foreign tourists . . .

Bobby Sounds ghastly . . .

Maisie Poor Hannah's gone straight to bed, in a state of collapse.

Bobby Great!

Maisie What . . .?

Bobby I mean—I'll have you all to myself (*He attempts to embrace her*) It's swell to see you again, Maisie . . .

Maisie (*evading him*) That's as may be, but I think you behaved disgracefully, leaving Hannah and me alone in London . . .

Bobby I was the one who was alone, baby.

Maisie Nonsense. We had masses of invitations, and you know how desperately Hannah needs a husband.

Bobby I'll tell you what she needs . . .

Maisie (*stopping him*) Now, Bobby, I may as well inform you that we are going straight back to London on the next plane . . .

Bobby Oh no, Maisie . . .

Maisie Oh, yes!

Bobby But, honey, now that you *are* here, can't we at least have a few days on our own? Say, come and have a look at the view . . .

He draws Maisie downstage

Look at that yacht. It's the President of Monomania's.

Maisie (*impressed*) Really?

Bobby And you know what? Tomorrow night he's coming to the re-opening of the *Café Pataplon*.

Maisie The *Café Pataplon*—(*softening*)—oh, Bobby . . .

Bobby (*taking her in his arms*) What do you say, Maisie?

Maisie I don't know . . . We have so many engagements in London. There's the Duchess of Putney's ball on Friday . . .

Bobby To hell with the Duchess. Say, how about a glass of champagne?

Maisie Well, it would revive me a little . . .

Bobby (*pouring two glasses*) Sure it would . . .

Maisie But the Marquis of Dorking is going to be there. He *is* sixty-five, but he's a widower and very lonely . . .

Bobby (*giving her a glass*) I've been lonely too, baby . . . Happy days!

Maisie Happy days!

Bobby And happy nights!

Maisie (*with a giggle*) Bobby . . .! (*She is about to drink when she notices something*) This glass has got lipstick on it!

Bobby (*innocently*) Really?

Maisie Yes! Look! I recognize the colour—Pink Flush!

Bobby What funny names they think of . . .

Maisie Bobby! Have you had a—a *woman* in here?

Bobby A woman? (*Laughing*) No! As a matter of fact . . .

Maisie So *that's* why you came to Nice!

Bobby Now, Maisie . . .

Maisie I might have known it!

Bobby Now, *Maisie* . . .!

Maisie Well, what have you got to say?

Bobby I—(*recalling what Polly has told him*)—I was just going to tell you that they don't do the washing-up very thoroughly in this hotel. Only this morning I had a coffee cup that was positively . . .

Maisie (*bursting into tears*) Oh! You—you monster!

Bobby But, Maisie . . .

Maisie I'm going straight to bed, and tomorrow we're going straight back to London. Or else . . .

She storms back inside and disappears C. *After a moment Bobby goes to the Brockhurst balcony*

Bobby (*calling softly*) Polly!

Polly (*re-appearing, in a negligée*) Yes?

Bobby I've done it too.

Polly Done what?

Bobby Made Maisie jealous—I think.

Polly Oh, Bobby . . .! How?

Bobby She found your lipstick on the champagne glass.

Polly Oh, dear . . . Do you think we've been wise?

Bobby I don't know. But—I've got hopes!

Tony (*off*) Polly!

Polly Yes, darling. Just coming.

Maisie (*very plaintively; off*) Bobby!

Bobby Yes, honey! With you in a minute!

Polly and Bobby wink at each other and go off to their respective suites

Tony (*off*) Polly, darling! I'm so sorry I . . .

Maisie (*with a giggle; off*) Oh . . . Bobby.

The Lights fade to Black-out

SCENE 4

The same. Next morning

Another chair has been set on each balcony

Cue No. 14.   *Music*

Solange and Raoul enter the Brockhurst and van Husen balcony respectively each carrying a breakfast tray with coffee for two. Each puts a cloth on the table, sets the tray and places two chairs upstage of the table. After completing this they exchange a surreptitious kiss over the parapet and Solange exits R *and Raoul exits* L

Tony enters from the Brockhurst suite, wearing pyjamas and dressing-gown, and looking very pleased with himself. He takes a few deep breaths and then sees the breakfast table

Tony (*calling*) Breakfast is served, madame!

Polly enters, wearing a negligée. Tony pours a cup of coffee and gives it to her

Polly Thank you, darling!

They kiss

No. 15   TOGETHER AGAIN

Tony	Darling, please forgive me For the things I said last night. I admit that I was wrong and you were right.
Polly	Why should I forgive you? For, as if you didn't know, I forgave you six or seven hours ago!
Tony	From now it's my intention We should be the perfect pair, And I hardly need to mention I'm so very glad that we're
	Together again, Together again, What matters is we are together again. As soon as you're near The clouds disappear And suddenly it's sunny weather again. We'll say our goodbyes To sorrows and sighs And promise to make a fresh start, And now that we're once more together again, We'll never again be apart.
Polly	Together again, Together again, What matters is we are together again. As soon as you're near The clouds disappear And suddenly it's sunny weather again. We'll say our goodbyes To sorrows and sighs And promise to make a fresh start,
Polly and Tony	And now that we're once more together again, We'll never again be apart.

They kiss again and exit to their suite

Maisie comes out on to the van Husen balcony, wearing a feathered negligée and looking radiant. She stretches luxuriantly and then sees the breakfast table

Maisie (*calling off*) Oh do get up, Bobby, and have your *petit déjeuner*! *She sits and pours the coffee*)

Bobby, wearing pyjamas and dressing-gown, enters yawning. He kisses Maisie and she gives him his coffee

Bobby Thanks, baby!
Maisie (*singing*) Darling, I'm so sorry
For the quarrel that we had,
When I had so little reason to be mad.
Bobby Honey, why be sorry
For a quarrel? If that's how
They would always end, let's have another now!
Maisie From this moment I've a feeling
That we'll be a perfect pair,
And there's no point in concealing
I'm so very glad that we're

Together again,
Together again,
What matters is we are together again.
As soon as you're near
The clouds disappear
Maisie and Bobby And suddenly it's sunny weather again.
We'll say our goodbyes
To sorrows and sighs
And promise to make a fresh start,
And now that we're once more together again,
We'll never again be apart.

Polly and Tony enter from their suite

Polly and Tony Together again,
Maisie and Bobby Together again,
Polly and Tony What matters is—
Maisie and Bobby   —we are—
Polly and Tony   —together—
Maisie and Bobby   —again.
Polly and Tony As soon as you're near
The clouds disappear
All And suddenly it's sunny weather again.
Polly We'll say our goodbyes
Maisie and Tony   —say our goodbyes
Polly To sorrows and sighs
Tony   —sorrows and sighs
All And promise to make a fresh start,
And now that we're once more together again,
We'll never again be apart.
And now that we're once more together again,
We'll never again be apart.

At the end of the song the two couples see each other and show great astonishment

Tony Well, I'm blowed, look who's here!
Maisie Why, it's Tony and Polly!
Bobby (*with exaggerated surprise*) Gee whiz! Of all the coincidences!

Polly (*with similar surprise*) Good heavens, it's Maisie and Bobby!

They greet each other warmly and have barely recovered from the "surprise" when Dulcie, Nancy and Fay enter the Brockhurst suite R

Dulcie Polly! Polly! (*She comes on to the balcony and stops dead*) No! I *don't* believe it . . .!

Fay (*joining her*) Nor do I!

Nancy (*coming on to the balcony*) What don't you believe . . .? Oh!

Dulcie, Nancy and Fay fall on Tony and Maisie with shrieks of delight when suddenly a loud voice is heard off stage from the direction of the van Husen suite. Everyone stops talking

Hannah, a brash lady in a colourful get-up with furs, enters the van Husen suite L

Hannah Doesn't anyone speak American round here? I'm looking for my brother, Bobby van Husen the Fourth . . .

Bobby Oh, no—Hannah!

Hannah (*coming on to the balcony*) Thank the Lord I've found you! This hotel is run entirely by foreigners!

Bobby It's a habit they have in France.

Hannah What? Say, who *are* all these people?

Maisie Everybody, this is Bobby's sister, Hannah. Hannah, isn't it extraordinary? We've all known each other for years!

Dulcie *Donkey's* years!

Maisie And we all arrived at the same hotel together.

Hannah That *is* extraordinary.

Dulcie And Bobby and Polly were next door to each other and didn't even know it!

Hannah (*significantly*) Is that so? Well, Maisie, extraordinary is hardly the word.

Maisie and Tony look stricken, remembering the events of the previous night

After a momentary pause Bobby and Polly are about to speak to Maisie and Tony respectively when Gaston and Hortense enter from the Brockhurst suite

Gaston *Pardon*, Monsieur Brockhurst, for this intrusion, but . . .

Tony (*angrily*) But what?

Hortense It is your *maman*, Lady Brockhurst . . .

Tony My *mother* . . .?

Lady Brockhurst (*off*) Where is my son? I demand to see my son!

She enters R *followed by Lord Brockhurst and Sir Freddy*

Lady Brockhurst There you are, Tony! Perhaps you can explain to these— (*with contempt*)—*French* individuals that once I have made camp I do not strike it until I am ready to move on!

Tony is dumbfounded

Gaston But, milady, the hotel gardens are private property!
Lady Brockhurst Stuff and nonsense! Take me to the British Consul at once!

They all start to argue. Hannah finds herself next to Sir Freddy downstage c

Hannah I don't think we've met.
Sir Freddy Er—no, I don't believe we have. I'm Fweddy ffothewington-ffitch.
Hannah (*incredulously*) Freddy *what?*
Sir Freddy ffothewington-ffitch. Sir Fweddy ffothewington-ffitch as a matter wof fact.
Hannah Did you say "Sir"?
Sir Freddy Yes. Bawonet actually.
Hannah Well—! (*Shaking his hand vigorously*) Pleased ter meetcher. My name's Hannah van Husen. *Miss* Hannah van Husen!

The noise suddenly increases. The shutters above fly open and Mme Dubonnet appears

Mme Dubonnet *Mesdames et Messieurs! Je vous en prie!* I am trying to sleep! Tonight I have to give a performance . . .!
Polly Who is that?
Hortense It is—Madame K!

Mme Dubonnet looks down, realizes she knows practically everyone and hurriedly puts on dark glasses

Raoul enters the Brockhurst suite as Solange enters the van Husen suite

Raoul
Solange } (*together*) { *Pardon!* 'Ave you finished breakfast?

A valet enters the van Husen suite and a chamber-maid enters the Brockhurst suite

Valet Monsieur would like his suit pressed?
Chamber-maid *Excusez-moi!* May I make the beds?

A manicurist enters the van Husen suite and a chef enters the Brockhurst suite

Manicurist Madame would like her nails polished?
Chef Monsieur would care to order luncheon?

All these requests fall of course on deaf ears. Hortense steps into the breach

Hortense Oh, *pardon*, but you see, this is all part of our service . . .

No. 16 PARADISE HOTEL (*Reprise*)

(*Singing*) All the guests must be so happy
When they fall beneath its spell
That the smart and the discerning
Ev'ry year will be returning

She nudges Gaston and he joins her

Hortense ⎫	
Gaston ⎬	To the Paradise Hotel.
Hortense ⎫	For the service is so snappy
Gaston ⎬	Ev'ry time you ring your bell
Staff ⎭	That we know that you'll donate a
	Tip to ev'ry maid and waiter
	At the Paradise Hotel!

On the last note all the Principals start arguing again. Mme Dubonnet throws up her hands in despair as—

the CURTAIN *falls*

ENTR'ACTE

ACT II

SCENE 1

Outside the Café Pataplon. That night

There is an entrance to the Café C, *with entrances* R *and* L

As the CURTAIN *rises, guests are entering the Café and being ushered in by the Manager*

Cue No. 17A. *Piano solo*

Alphonse, Marcel and Pierre, wearing tails, enter L, *on the look-out for girls and go off again* R

Bobby, also in tails, enters L *with Maisie and Hannah who are both wearing dance frocks*

Maisie Oh, Bobby, doesn't it look utterly different?
Bobby Sure does! But I guess we do too, honey.
Hannah (*indulgently*) Nonsense! You're still my kid brother to me.
Bobby Aw, Hannah, please . . .
Hannah Oh yes, you are! Why, look at you now—coming out on a chilly evening without your silk scarf!
Bobby What scarf?

Tony enters R *and overhears Hannah*

Hannah What scarf? You know very well what scarf. The one I gave you with your initial on it, which I embroidered with my very own hands: R for Robert.
Bobby Oh gee, I don't know, Hannah. I guess I didn't bring it with me . . .
Hannah You sure did! I put it into your suitcase myself . . .

They continue arguing as Polly enters R. *Tony is drawing his own conclusions*

Polly Oh look, darling—there are Bobby and Maisie.
Tony Polly, I want to have a word with you . . .
Bobby (*extricating himself*) Look, there are Polly and Tony! Let's team up . . .

Maisie and Tony both hang back

Hannah (*greeting Polly*) Say, Mrs Brockhurst, don't you look a picture? Mr Honourable Brockhurst should be proud of you!
Polly (*modestly*) Oh—thank you.

Hannah And that's a gorgeous lipstick you're wearing. Isn't it that new shade—what's its name? Maisie, *you* know. When *I* wear it, I look like a slice of water-melon . . .

Bobby urges Maisie and Hannah UC

Bobby Say, shouldn't we be going in? It's nearly eight o'clock.
Polly Yes, we should . . .
Hannah I've got it—Pink Flush!
Maisie Pink Flush! (*Catching Bobby's arm*) Bobby, I want to have a word with you . . .

She draws him aside

Tony (*taking Polly aside*) Now, Polly, listen to me . . .
Hannah Hey, what's going on? Aren't we gonna have dinner? I'm so hungry I could eat *à la carte* and the horse as well!
Maisie That *was* the same lipstick on that champagne glass!

Hannah tries to overhear. Maisie lowers her voice and continues talking angrily to Bobby

Tony R stands for Robert. And Robert is short for Bobby!

Hannah moves over to Tony. He also lowers his voice. Hannah shrugs and moves C

No. 18   DIVORCE ME, DARLING

Polly	Well, all right—
Bobby	Well, all right—
Polly ⎫ **Bobby** ⎭	Apropos of what happened last night . . .
Polly	If you believe I've been untrue to you, Divorce me, darling!
	For nowadays it's very simple to Divorce me, darling.
	And if my virtue is in doubt,
Bobby	Then there is only one way out,
Polly	Divorce me, darling!
Bobby	Divorce me, darling!
Polly ⎫ **Bobby** ⎭	Divorce me, darling! And I assure you there will be no need To force me, darling, Cos I shall only be too ready to agree You'll see. So if you want to live alone, Just get the lawyer on the phone, And let's arrange when the happy day will be.

Alphonse, Marcel and Pierre enter R

Marcel Alphonse, Pierre! *Regardez! C'est* Maisie!

Alphonse ⎱
Pierre   ⎰ *(together)* ⎰ Maisie!

They rush and surround Maisie, much to her astonishment. She is caught between distress at the thought of divorce and her customary enjoyment of flattery

The music continues and Dulcie, Fay and Nancy enter L

Dulcie Hello, Polly! Here we are at last. Is something up?

Polly is at a loss

(*Seeing the husbands*) Nancy! Fay! Look! Our *husbands*!
Alphonse Marcel! Pierre! *Regardez*! Our *wives*!
Wives What are you doing here? You're supposed to be in Paris!
Husbands *Qu'est ce que tu fais ici?* You are supposed to be in *Angleterre*!

Maisie ⎫	There's a spot of trouble brewing
Tony and ⎬	And I'll never be at peace
Husbands ⎭	Till I know what you've been doing
	In the wicked town of Nice.
Bobby ⎫	If you're jumping to conclusions,
Polly and ⎬	Then go on and jump, my friend,
Wives ⎭	But be under no delusions,
	On the rocks is where we'll end,
	High and dry and washed up matrimonially.
Maisie ⎱	
Tony ⎰	Oh, no!
Alphonse	*Mais non!*
Marcel	*Mais non!*
Pierre	*Mais non!*
Bobby ⎫	
Polly and ⎬	*Mais oui!*
Wives ⎭	
Nancy	If you believe I've gone astray, then do
All	Divorce me, darling.
Fay	As I presume you feel the same way too,
All	Divorce me, darling.
Dulcie	And just to make it all complete,
	Your little wifey will repeat
All	Divorce me, darling,
	Divorce me, darling,
	Divorce me, darling.
	If in the marriage race you're anxious to
	Unhorse me, darling,
	Then I am perfectly prepared to set you free
	From me.
Nancy	I'll simply say "Ta ta, old sport",

| | And I'll be seeing you in court, |
| **All** | And let's arrange when the happy day will be. |

Fay	And just to coin a brand new phrase,
	We've reached the parting of the ways,
All	And let's arrange when the happy day will be.

Dulcie	But there's no need to bear a grudge,
	We'll simply tell it to the judge,
All	And he'll arrange when the happy day will be.

The Manager enters C

Manager *Mesdames, messieurs! Je vous en prie! Silence pour Monsieur le Président!*

They all shut up reluctantly

Cue No. 19. *Anthem*

The President—or rather Percy in disguise—appears L. *The ladies curtsy and the men bow. Percy gives a start of surprise on seeing Polly, but pulls himself together and goes into the Café*

As soon as he is gone the argument breaks out afresh and everyone exits C *except Hannah who remains alone on stage*

No. 20   HERE AM I

Hannah They're all talking about divorces,
But they're all way ahead.
I'm not talking about divorces
Cos I've not even been wed.
In fact the situation makes me see red.
Well, if you look at it my way . . .

Here am I,
But where's the guy
Who'll make my life complete?
I look down every street
But all the men I see
Somehow don't see me.

How I long
For someone strong
To hot up my heart-beat.
But ev'ry time that I spot him
Some other dame has already got him.

I don't ask for much, my friends.
I just want my rights.
I yearn for the touch, my friends,
That lights up the lights
On those dark winter nights.

So here I'll stay
And come what may,
I'll know before I die
The thrill of suddenly saying
"Here am I and there's my guy!"

The chorus is repeated musically and Hannah attempts to get off with other gentlemen entering the Café, but they all have partners

An American sailor enters on his own and Hannah vamps him. They dance together

So—here I'll stay,
And come what may,
I'll know before I die
The thrill of suddenly saying,
"Here am I,
Here am I,
Here am I, and there's my guy!"

After the applause, Sir Freddy enters L. On seeing him, Hannah dismisses the sailor, who exits R

(*Enticingly*) Why . . . hullo!

Sir Freddy Oh—Miss van Husen, isn't it?

Hannah That's right, Sir Baronet. But won't you call me Hannah?

Sir Freddy Why? Is that your name?

Hannah Well, it ain't Betty Boop. Yours is Freddy, I believe.

Sir Freddy How did you know? Oh of course, I told you, didn't I? I am a silly ass.

Hannah I don't think so. Say—are you going any place?

Sir Freddy Any place . . .? Oh, you mean anywhere!

Hannah Anywhere's all right with me. How about here?

Sir Freddy Well, I don't know what Aunt Hilda would say. We're supposed to be giving an exhibition in some westauwaument—and I can't wemember which.

Hannah Well, let's go and make an exhibition of ourselves here, huh?

Sir Freddy All wight—I say, are you an Amewican?

Hannah Yeah, kiddo—Howdja know?

She propels him inside C, as Hortense enters with Gaston R, both in evening dress

Hortense Oh, Monsieur Gaston, I have not been here since the night of the Carnival Ball, all those years ago. I wore a peasant dress belonging to *ma mère* . . .

Gaston *Vraiment? Ah, ma chère*, at the next Carnival Ball you will wear a mink coat!

Hortense *Oh, là là!*

Mme Dubonnet enters C, in a state of distress. She wears an evening-gown and furs

Mme Dubonnet Ah, Hortense! Thank goodness I have found you!

Hortense What is it, madame? You look *bouleversée!*

Mme Dubonnet Polly—she is in the audience—with her husband. I cannot go on . . .

Hortense But surely, madame, after what you told me yesterday: night after night you have got to go on, though your heart . . .

Mme Dubonnet No, Hortense, no! Think of the disgrace! To have to realize, in front of all her friends, that her step-mother is—a Cabaret Star!

Hortense Is there anything I can do?

Mme Dubonnet (*after a moment*) Yes, Hortense—there is! Go on in my place.

Hortense Oh no, madame . . .

Mme Dubonnet No-one here has ever seen me before, and you can wear a mask.

Hortense Perhaps . . . But even so—I—to go on instead of you—I would not dare, madame. It would be unthinkable, impossible . . . (*With a change of tone*) What shall I sing?

Mme Dubonnet I knew I could rely on you. (*Taking her hand*) Quick, quick, there is no time to waste!

Hortense (*hanging back*) Oh, madame! Oh, Gaston! Oh dear . . .!

Mme Dubonnet *Courage, ma petite!* Remember . . . (*She sings*)

No. 21   LIGHTS! MUSIC! (*Reprise*)

> Up off your knees,
> For the Theatre decrees
> It's lights! Music!

Hortense (*falteringly*) Lights! Music!

All   Lights! Music!
                             And on with the show!

They all exit L

Cue No. 21b.   *Fanfare*

Manager (*off*) *Monsieur le Président, mesdames et messieurs*, it gives me great pleasure to welcome you to the *Nouveau Café Pataplon.*

There is the sound of applause off

Cue No. 22.   *Music*

Maisie enters C, *crying. After a moment Bobby follows her*

Bobby Maisie, honey . . .

Maisie I—don't want to talk to you.

Bobby But, baby . . .

Maisie There's nothing more to say. If—if you want a divorce, you can have one.

Bobby Now listen . . .

Maisie Don't you understand plain English? I—do—not—wish—to—talk—to—you!

Bobby shrugs his shoulders and is about to enter the Café. An idea strikes him and he starts a very soft tap dance to the music. At first against her will, Maisie joins in, and gradually they start dancing together

No. 22   OUT OF STEP

Bobby When I'm out of step with you
The whole world goes cock-eyed too,
And the music's just an empty refrain.
Oh, my darling, let's get in step again!

When you're out of step with me,
The whole evening seems to be
Nothing but a catastrophical bore.
Oh, my darling, let's get in step once more!

Because when
We're in step,
I can feel our hearts take wing,
And then
Ev'ry step
Has a beat to make the angels sing.

We were out of step, I know,
But you're close to me and, oh,
I can catch a glimpse of heaven in view,
Cos it's heaven when I'm in step with you!

(Second ending)

Cos it's heaven when I'm in step—
Oh, my darling, let's get in step—
It's sheer heaven when I'm in step with you!

There is an Encore, during which the scene changes to the interior of the Café Pataplon, where everyone is dancing

SCENE 2

The Interior of the Café Pataplon. Immediately following

There is a curtained entrance UC *and entrances* R *and* L. *Tables and chairs placed* U *and at the sides form a surround to the dance floor* C

Percy is seated alone at a table UL *watching the couples dancing. At the end of the dance, Polly runs over to Bobby, closely watched by Tony and Maisie*

Polly Bobby! I must talk to you! I honestly think we went too far . . .
Maisie *(overhearing)* Too far? Oh . . .! *(She bursts into tears)*

Bobby Hey, Maisie . . .!

Polly Oh dear, I've made it worse . . .

Bobby (*putting his arm round her shoulder*) It'll be O.K., Polly—just remember last night.

Tony (*overhearing*) Now, look here, van Husen . . .!

There is a drum roll. The Manager calls for silence and everyone settles down reluctantly, facing away from each other

Manager *Monsieur le Président, mesdames, messieurs*, the *Nouveau Café Pataplon* takes great pleasure in presenting for your entertainment the renowned star of International Cabaret—Madame K!

Everyone applauds

Cue No. 23. *Music introduction to "Fancy Forgetting"*

The "President" appears very moved

Hortense enters very hesitantly from UC. *She is wearing a mask*

No. 23   FANCY FORGETTING

Hortense Fancy forgetting the love that we knew
When we were fancy free.
Fancy forgetting what I said to you
And what you said to me.
Though the years go by
And our youth is gone,
Memories don't die,
Like a song they linger on.
So just when I thought you'd remember it too . . .

Percy (*jumping to his feet*) No . . .!

There is consternation

Manager (*running to Percy*) *Monsieur le Président*—is something wrong?

Percy I cannot be party to this deception. That lady is *not* Madame K! (*He removes Hortense's mask*)

Everyone is riveted

Mme Dubonnet enters from UC

Mme Dubonnet (*singing*) Fancy, just fancy you forgetting.

Percy is overwhelmed

(*Speaking*) Yes, *Monsieur le Président*, it is true. This lady is not Madame K. (*To Hortense*) Thank you, Hortense, you did your best.

Hortense (*retiring*) It was nothing, madame.

Mme Dubonnet But I think this is not the only deception to be practised here tonight!

There is further consternation. Polly has recognized Mme Dubonnet

(*To Percy*) You are *not* the President of Monomania!

Percy (*after a struggle with his conscience*) It is true! I can't pretend any longer! (*Tearing off his beard*) Kiki!

Mme Dubonnet Percy!

Polly Daddy!

Dulcie I say, everyone, it's Madame Dubonnet and Polly's father!

Percy, Mme Dubonnet and Polly embrace, to everyone's delight

Manager And now, *mesdames et messieurs*, I have great pleasure in presenting *la vraie Madame K*—the *true* Madame Kiki!

Percy joins Polly at her table. Mme Dubonnet is about to perform when singing is heard off stage

> *Lady Brockhurst enters* L, *marching, followed by Cecelia, Prunella and Felicity, who are all wearing PT outfits. Lord Brockhurst, dressed in tails, follows in behind them*

Lady Brockhurst Squadron—halt!

Sir Freddy Oh Lord, it *was* this westauwant!

Lady Brockhurst Deserter! Take your place in the ranks!

Hannah Hey, wait a moment! He's with me!

Lady Brockhurst A Yankee! I might have known it!

Lord Brockhurst (*sotto voce to Sir Freddy*) Not bad, me boy. A bit broad in the beam, but looks as if she's got plenty of staying power!

Sir Freddy *And* plenty of the weady!

Lord Brockhurst Good show!

Lady Brockhurst (*blowing her whistle*) Silence! Squadron! Take up positions!

The girls, Lord Brockhurst and Sir Freddy form a tableau

Manager Madame, if you please . . .!

Lady Brockhurst Out of my way, my good man! Ladies and gentlemen, my group and I will now show you a few basic movements.

Hannah This should be interesting!

Lady Brockhurst And—one, and two and three and four, and one and two and three and four . . .

They perform a grotesque Swedish Drill. Suddenly there is a loud report, followed by a cloud of smoke which envelops the President's table and Lady Brockhurst. When it clears, the Manager picks up the remains of a champagne bottle

Manager The champagne! It must have contained a bomb!

Mme Dubonnet Percy! Someone tried to kill you!

Percy Not me—the President!

> *The President enters* C, *wearing a black broad-brimmed hat and wrapped in a black cloak*

President (*throwing aside his cloak*) Yes, my friend, that is the case. And thanks to your bravery in taking my place, I have been able to uncover the conspiracy and apprehend the culprit. I was hoping to arrive in time to prevent the explosion, but, *gracias a Dios*, no-one has been hurt—has she?

Suddenly everyone notices the absence of Lady Brockhurst

Lord Brockhurst Good Lord! Where's the wife?

Lady Brockhurst (*a muffled voice from under the wreckage*) Hubert! Hubert! Where *are* you?

Lord Brockhurst (*aside*) Thought it was too good to be true . . .(*Aloud*) Coming, m'dear!

With the aid of Tony and Sir Freddy, Lord Brockhurst extricates Lady Brockhurst who emerges with a smoke-blackened face and her clothes in tatters

Lady Brockhurst (*rising to her feet*) This means war!

President Ah no, señora. I can explain . . .

Lady Brockhurst And who, may I ask, are you?

Percy This, Lady Brockhurst, is the President of Monomania.

Lady Brockhurst (*to Percy*) Polly's father! I thought you were in South America, evading justice.

Mme Dubonnet That is not true! He was innocent!

Percy You knew that, Kiki?

Mme Dubonnet Of course I did, Percy.

All (*touched*) Ahhhh!

Percy And now, Señor President? I can tell you my real name. It is not Jones. It is Browne.

Hortense Browne *avec un "e"*!

Lady Brockhurst What *is* going on, Hubert? I demand to know the truth!

President It is rather a long story, señora. May I suggest that since this unfortunate incident has caused some damage—(*to the Manager*)—for which I shall of course re-imburse you, señor, that we continue the Gala aboard my yacht.

Everyone cheers and applauds. Lady Brockhurst blows her whistle

Lady Brockhurst Hubert!

Lord Brockhurst Oh—er—coming, m'dear!

Lady Brockhurst Frederick! We are waiting!

Sir Freddy (*to Hannah*) Vewy sowwy, Miss van Husen, but I'm afwaid . . .

Hannah Hey, wait a minute, Baronet. You haven't even got my phone number!

Lady Brockhurst Squadron! Quick—march!

Lady Brockhurst, Ceceila, Prunella, Felicity, Freddy and Lord Brockhurst march off L to music as the scene changes

SCENE 3

The Promenade des Anglais. A moment later

As the Front cloth comes in, Percy moves forward, with his arms round Polly and Mme Dubonnet

Percy My beloved wife! My beloved daughter!

No. 24 TOGETHER AGAIN (*Reprise*)

(*Singing*)	I'm so very glad that we're Together again
Mme Dubonnet **Polly** }	Together again
All	What matters is we are together again.
Mme Dubonnet	As soon as you're near The clouds disappear
All	And suddenly it's sunny weather again We'll say our goodbyes To sorrows and sighs And promise to make a fresh start, And now that we're once more together again . . .

On the last words Polly breaks off and looks away. The music continues softly

Percy Polly—are you hiding something?
Mme Dubonnet Let me have a word with her.

Mme Dubonnet draws Polly aside

  Chère Polly, what is making you unhappy?
Polly It's nothing really—just a silly misunderstanding. I could explain everything to Tony in a minute—if only he'd *listen*.
Mme Dubonnet Then we must *make* him listen! Percy!

Mme Dubonnet gestures Percy to go ahead and, taking Polly's arm, follows

  All will be well, *ma chère*. You will see!

Mme Dubonnet, Polly and Percy exit. The music swells and then stops

Lord and Lady Brockhurst, now in evening dress, enter R

Lady Brockhurst But, Hubert, why should you wish to attend this wretched Gala? Especially after what I have just been through.
Lord Brockhurst We ought to celebrate. It's not every evening that somebody tries to blow you up—(*sotto voce*)—more's the pity.
Lady Brockhurst What did you say, Hubert?
Lord Brockhurst (*gesturing at the view*) I said, "Awfully pretty".

Sir Freddy enters R, *looking disconsolate*

  There's young Freddy. Why don't you go and—admire the view, m'dear? I want to have a word with him.

Lady Brockhurst (*reluctantly*) Oh—very well. (*She moves away* L)
Lord Brockhurst Freddy! I say, Freddy, m'boy!
Sir Freddy Yes, Uncle?
Lord Brockhurst What have you done with her?
Sir Freddy Who, Uncle?
Lord Brockhurst That American filly—she's too good to lose.
Sir Freddy I know, but Aunt Hilda wouldn't appwove. She thinks Amewicans are vulgar.
Lord Brockhurst So they are—dashed vulgar. But beggars can't be choosers.
Sir Freddy That's twue.
Lord Brockhurst (*looking off* R) Here she comes now.
Sir Freddy But—but what will Aunt Hilda say?
Lord Brockhurst B—*bother* Aunt Hilda!
Lady Brockhurst (*coming towards them*) Hubert! I heard that!
Lord Brockhurst (*taking her arm*) Did you, m'dear? What big ears you have!

Hannah enters R

(*Gesturing to Sir Freddy*) There you are, Freddy! Attaboy!

Lady Brockhurst Hubert! Have you been drinking?
Lord Brockhurst (*propelling his wife along*) No, but it's high time we started!

Lord and Lady Brockhurst exit L

Sir Freddy Whatever did he mean by that?
Hannah If you really don't know, Sir Freddy, it's high time you started learning.

She grabs him and kisses him enthusiastically

Sir Freddy (*dazed*) Good gwacious!
Hannah Did you enjoy it?
Sir Freddy Yes, by George, I did! I say—attagirl!

He grabs her and kisses her back

No. 25   YOU'RE ABSOLUTELY ME

Hannah   I've not met Mahatma Ghandi,
                   I don't drink Napoleon Brandy,
                   So I can't compare them to you.
Sir Freddy   I've not seen the Mona Lisa
                   Or the leaning tower of Pisa,
                   So for me the same holds twue.
Hannah   I've heard such things are high praise
                   So my praise
                   Sounds low.
                   All I can do
                   Is liken you

	To things I really know.
	For instance—
	You're a strong Manhattan
Sir Freddy	You're a gin and it.
Hannah	You're a tune that's Latin.
Sir Freddy	You're the latest hit
	Played in Charlie Kunz's fav'rite key,
	Which goes to show you're absolutely me.
Hannah	You're a Crawford weepie.
Sir Freddy	You're a Hulbert flick.
Hannah	You're a Karloff creepie
Sir Freddy	You're the whole Old Vic.
Hannah	You're a coloured Silly Symphony,
	Which means to say you're absolutely me.
	You're fruit and nut.
Sir Freddy	You're shaggy cut.
Hannah	You're Crosby on the mike.
	You're Boston beans.
Sir Freddy	You're tinned sardines.
Both	You're ev'rything I like.
Sir Freddy	You're a brace of pheasant.
Hannah	You're an oyster stew.
Sir Freddy	You are Wilton Crescent
Hannah	You're Fifth Avenue
	Where I'll take you on a shopping spree.
Sir Freddy	Oh, yes, my dear, that's absolutely me!
Hannah	You're the Isle of Coney.
Sir Freddy	You're a stick of rock.
	You're a Shetland pony.
Hannah	You're a floral clock
	In the Spring in Washington DC,
	Which means to say you're absolutely me.
Sir Freddy	You're a toasted tea-cake
Hannah	You're a pumpkin pie.
Sir Freddy	You're a rich Dundee cake.
Hannah	You're a ham on rye.
Sir Freddy	You're tomato sauce, also HP
	Which goes to show you're absolutely me.
	You're Ovaltine.
Hannah	You're gasoline.
Sir Freddy	You're cold stewed prunes and rice.
Hannah	You're aged in wood.
Sir Freddy	You're Yorkshire pud.
Both	You're ev'rything that's nice.
Sir Freddy	You're Westminster Abbey.
Hannah	You're the Empire State.
Sir Freddy	You're a cat that's tabby.
Hannah	You're a Dane that's great.

> You are everything you wanna be.
> Because, my dear, you're absolutely,

Sir Freddy Absolutely, definitely,
Both Definitely, absolutely me!

Sir Freddy and Hannah exit R *and then re-enter*

YOU'RE ABSOLUTELY ME (*Reprise*)

Hannah You're a suit that's natty.
Sir Freddy You are Harris tweeds.
Hannah You're Carnegie, Hattie.
Sir Freddy You are Austin Reeds.
Hannah You're the whole darn chain of A and P,
And that's because you're absolutely me.
Sir Freddy You're a Baby Austin.
Hannah Not a Rolls? Aw, shucks!
You're a fur coat costin'
Sev'ral thousand bucks.
Sir Freddy Sev'ral thousand bucks I'd like to see.
Hannah You will because you're absolutely me.
Sir Freddy You're Droitwich Spa.
Hannah You're Florida.
Sir Freddy You're Simla and Cawnpore.
Hannah You're corned-beef hash.
Sir Freddy You're sausage'n mash.
Both You're all that I adore.
Sir Freddy You're a pound of bulls' eyes
In an air-tight tin.
Hannah You're a photo full-size
Of the Roosevelt grin.
What I mean to say is, we agree
You're definitely,
Sir Freddy Absolutely,
Hannah Absolutely,
Sir Freddy Definitely,
Both Definitely, absolutely me!

Sir Freddy and Hannah exit L *and the Lights fade to Black-out*

SCENE 4

On board the President's Yacht. Later that night

The front cloth goes up to reveal the President's yacht. The bridge runs across up stage with entrances R *and* L. *There is a companionway* C *from the bridge to the stage. There are entrances upstage and downstage* R *and* L. *The yacht is hung with bunting and coloured lights*

Cue No. 26. *Music introduction to "Back Where We Started"*

48   Divorce Me, Darling!

Nancy and Pierre are standing together on the bridge C, *Dulcie and Alphonse
are* UR *and Fay and Marcel are* DL. *Polly stands alone* DR

Percy and Tony enter L

Percy Polly . . .
Polly Yes, Daddy?
Percy I think Tony has something to say to you.

He gestures Tony over to Polly

Tony (*taking her hands*) I'm sorry, Polly. I've been a fool . . .
Polly Oh no, Tony, it was all my fault.
Tony No, Polly. I just put two and two together . . .
Polly And made the worst kind of four? Oh, don't apologize, Tony. I
wanted you to be jealous.
Tony Well, I was—I assure you!
Polly Oh, darling . . .

*Polly melts into Tony's arms with a grateful look at Percy, who waves
and exits* L

Isn't it funny?
Tony Funny?
Polly We had to come all the way back to Nice to find out how much we
really cared . . .

No. 26   BACK WHERE WE STARTED

Here we are
Back where we started,
Just as much
In love as before.
Who could tell
When we were parted
Fate would engage
Us to stage
An encore?
For
Just a while
I was downhearted.
Life was vile
And love was in vain.
But oh, I ought to know
How near we are.
All I did was call
And here we are
Back where we started
In love again.

Tony   Isn't it strange how fate arranges things,
                 Constantly taking us by surprise?
Polly   Just when we least expect, she changes things,

	Constantly making us realize

Constantly making us realize
How much we owe to chance,
In spite of our resistance.

Tony A smile, a sigh, a glance
Can change our whole existence.

Both And so we know it must be right
That Fate has led us where we are tonight,
For . . .

The chorus is repeated in which the Husbands and Wives join

At the end of the song everyone exits with the exception of Dulcie

Lord Brockhurst enters R

Lord Brockhurst Hello, hello, hello! Not feeling fed up with France, eh?

Dulcie Oh, Lord Brockhurst, tonight I'm absolutely not fed up with anything!

No. 26A BACK WHERE WE STARTED (*Reprise*)

Both Here we are
Back where we started,
Having fun
As we did before.
Who could tell
When we were parted
Fate would engage
Us to stage
An encore?
For
Just a while
We were downhearted,
Life was vile
And full of ennui.
But though today it may seem stupid to
Still say "wack-a-doo" and "boop-a-doo",
Back where we started we're glad to be,
Back where we started we're glad to be—

Dulcie (*speaking*) —one more time—

Both (*singing*) Back where we started we're glad to be.

Dulcie and Lord Brockhurst exit DR

Bobby enters UR as Polly enters DL

Polly Oh, Bobby, I've been looking for you everywhere. Tony knows what really happened and everything's all right!

Maisie enters on the bridge from L

Bobby (*patting Polly's arm*) Say, that's great! Now I gotta find Maisie and put things right with her.

Polly Yes, do!

The yacht gives a sudden lurch, and Polly is thrown into Bobby's arms, at which moment Maisie looks down and sees them

Maisie (*bursting into tears*) Ohhhhhh!

Maisie runs off L. *Bobby runs off after her but bumps into Nancy and Pierre who are coming down the companionway from* R *before he exits* L. *The other Guests drift on*

There is a drum roll and a spot appears on the bridge

Nancy Whatever's happening now?
Pierre Sssh! It's Madame K!

Mme Dubonnet enters on the bridge L. *She wears an immaculate naval officer's uniform and is smoking a cigarette in a short holder. She comes* C *and begins the song, moving down the companionway and on to the stage as she sings*

No. 27   BLONDES FOR DANGER

Mme Dubonnet I've travelled the seven seas
From Frisco to Hong Kong
And I have learned a lot along the way.
I've done what I darn'd well please
And sometimes I've gone wrong,
But I'm alive to tell the tale today.
So when I see those fresh young sailors
Come ashore from off their ships,
I feel inclined
To say, "D'you mind
If I offer you some tips?"
And if I should see one stare
At a girl with golden hair,
I tap him on the shoulder and say:

Beware, young stranger,
Don't you know it's Blondes for Danger?
When a blonde appears, get ready for action.
Beware, young fellow,
Of a girl whose hair is yellow,
Yellow hair can drive a man to distraction.
And if you choose her,
You are sure to be the loser.
Fair-haired ladies very rarely play fair.

You can make a household pet
Of a red-head or brunette;
But it's Blondes for Danger,
So, stranger, beware.

I'm telling you straight, young stranger,

> Before it's too late, young stranger,
> Don't trifle with Fate, young stranger,

(speaking) Just beware,

The ensemble join, bouche fermée, as the chorus is repeated

(singing)   . . . young stranger
>   Don't you know it's Blondes for Danger?
>   When a blonde appears, get ready for action.
>   Beware, young fellow,
>   Of a girl whose hair is yellow,
>   Yellow hair can drive a man to distraction.
>   And if you choose her,
>   You are sure to be the loser.
>   Fair-haired ladies very rarely play fair——
(speaking) —and square.
(Singing)   You can make a household pet
>   Of a red-head or brunette;
>   But it's Blondes for Danger,
>   So, stranger, beware.

After the applause, the President enters on the bridge from L *and calls for silence*

President (*coming down the companionway*) Señoras and *Caballeros!* Welcome aboard! And now, before the dancing, she commence, I wish to express my thanks to a brave and faithful *amigo*. (*Producing a scroll*) Señor Browne, come and claim your reward!

Percy comes forward and receives the scroll, as everyone applauds

Percy (*unrolling it*) Why, this is—this is . . .
Mme Dubonnet What is it, Percy?
Percy The deed of ownership of the Monomanian Platinum Mine—the proof of my innocence!

He is about to hand it back to the President

President No, no, keep it. It is yours!
Mme Dubonnet Percy! Your fortune is made once more!
Percy *Our* fortune, you mean. Kiki, you need no longer be a Cabaret Star.
Lady Brockhurst (*firmly*) I'm delighted to hear it!

The President, Percy and Mme Dubonnet exit UL

The music starts and everyone dances

> *Bobby enters, looking for Maisie, and immediately Hannah leads Sir Freddy over to meet him*

Hannah Say, Bobby, look what I'm taking home to momma!
Bobby Yeah?
Hannah Yeah! We're gonna be married—aren't we, Freddy?

Sir Freddy We sure are!

Hannah Why don't you congratulate us? Your big sister's gonna be a lady at last!

Bobby That's great, Hannah. But I'm trying to find Maisie . . .

Bobby exits UR

The music stops and a burst of giggles can be heard off R

Cecelia, Prunella and Felicity run on DR, *followed by three American sailors. The girls still wear shorts, but have put on sailor hats and tap shoes*

Lady Brockhurst Gels! What is the meaning of this?

Cecelia Oh, Lady Brockhurst, we're terribly sorry, but we somehow bumped into these chaps!

Lady Brockhurst So I see!

Prunella And they've been teaching us a new Movement!

Felicity It's even bigger than Health and Beauty!

Lady Brockhurst Impossible!

Cecelia Oh, but it is. Tell her, boys!

Sailors Sure! We'd be glad to!

No. 28   SWING TIME IS HERE TO STAY

            Do you hear that sound?

Girls   Yes, I hear that sound!

Sailors Do you hear that beat
            Of those tapping feet?
            Well, that's the beat that's the latest thing,
            That's the sound of Swing!

Maisie appears on the bridge C. *She is wearing an abbreviated admiral's uniform, with navy blue sequins and silver braid*

Maisie It's a new beat
            That's not a blue beat,
            It's hi-de-do-hi-de-hey.
            Ev'rybody's in Swing Time,
            Swing Time is here to stay.

            Goodbye, bad news,
            For here's the glad news,
            The Jubilee's on its way.
            Ev'rybody's in Swing Time,
            Swing Time is here to stay.
            From the Sunny South to the Frozen North
            Ev'ryone's learning to Swing,
            And on New Year's Eve or July the Fourth
            Swing is the thing,
            Swing is King!

            We've had a session
            Of sad depression,

But now we're all going gay,
Ev'rybody's in Swing Time,
Swing Time is here to stay—
I wanna tell you—
Swing Time is here to stay!

This leads into a dance number involving the whole company

Bobby enters to dance with Maisie, and Percy and Mme Dubonnet, now in evening dress, enter and join in

We've had a session of sad depression,
But now we're all going gay.
Ev'rybody's in Swing Time,
Swing Time is here to stay!
All   In whatever country you chance to be,
You'll see them learning to Swing,
And in London, New York and Gay Paree
Swing is the thing,
Swing is King!

The world rejoices,
So raise your voices,
Let's hear that hip-hip-hooray!
Ev'rybody's in Swing Time,
Swing Time is here to stay!

After the applause Bobby joins Maisie and Polly and Tony follow him

Bobby Maisie, honey, you've *gotta* listen to me! Polly and I just had one drink together last night—nothing more.
Polly It's true, Maisie.

Tony nods agreement

Maisie *(coolly)* Honestly? *(Suddenly embracing Bobby)* Oh, Bobby, darling, why didn't you *tell* me?
Dulcie *(joining them)* Oh, I say, Maisie! Polly! It's all too marvellous! We've decided *not* to get divorced after all!

The other Wives and Husbands reiterate this

So now we can all have a simply topping time together—just like the old days!

Suddenly Polly faints, Tony catching her

Tony Polly! What's the matter?

In quick succession, Maisie, Dulcie, Nancy and Fay faint into the arms of Bobby, Alphonse, Pierre and Marcel

Bobby Maisie! What's wrong?
Alphonse Dulcie! *Qu'est que c'est?*
Pierre Nancy! *Es-tu malade?*

Marcel Fay! *Dis-moi quelque-chose!*
Mme Dubonnet *Tiens, tiens!* Give them some air!
Polly (*coming round*) Where am I?
Tony Are you all right, darling?
Polly (*recovering*) Oh yes—really. It's just—I've been meaning to tell you, Tony, but . . .
Tony You don't mean . . .?

Polly nods

Oh, Polly, this is marvellous!

Meanwhile, the other Wives have also recovered and revealed the same secret to their Husbands

Bobby Maisie, this is great!
Alphonse Dulcie . . .
Pierre Nancy . . .
Marcel Fay . . .
Husbands *C'est formidable!*
Lord Brockhurst (*slapping Lady Brockhurst on the back*) D'you hear that, You're going to be a granny!
Lady Brockhurst What—again?
Hannah (*to Sir Freddy*) And you're gonna be an uncle—as soon as we get married.
Sir Freddy Oh—weally?
Gaston Married? *Alors*, you know where to spend your honeymoon!
Hannah No. Where?
Hortense Where I am spending mine—(*nudging Gaston*)—at the Paradise Hotel.
Wives / **Husbands** } (*together*) { Of course! Let's all do the same!

No. 29 DIVORCE ME, DARLING (*Finale*)

Husbands Let's have a honeymoon instead of a Divorce, my darling. Let's have it right away— Is that okay?
Wives Of course, my darling! And I would like to make it plain You'll never hear me say again Divorce me, darling! Divorce me, darling! Divorce me, darling!
Husbands If I'm the gander, you're the goose to share My sauce, my darling.
Wives And very soon we will be four Where we were three, You'll see!

All	As soon as we are on our own,
	We'll get the doctor on the phone
	And he'll announce
	And he'll announce
	And he'll announce when the happy day will be!

CURTAIN

Act II, Scene 4

All   'As soon as we are on our own,
        We'll get the doctor on the phone
        And he'll announce
        And he'll announce

FURNITURE AND PROPERTY LIST

PROLOGUE

On stage: Nil

Personal: **Dulcie:** wristwatch

ACT I

SCENE 1

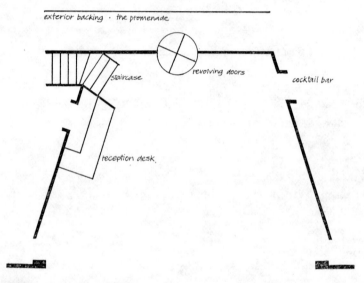

exterior backing · the promenade

staircase

revolving doors

cocktail bar

reception desk

On stage: Reception desk. *On it:* telephone, hand-bell, hotel register, pen-stand

Off stage: Several suitcases **(Bell-boy)**
Small suitcase **(Dulcie)**
Small suitcase **(Nancy)**
Small suitcase **(Fay)**
Two suitcases (with monogram PB), hat-box **(Bell-boy)**

SCENE 2

On stage: Nil

Off stage: Five placards which read: HEALTH AND BEAUTY **(Lady Brockhurst, Cecelia, Felicity, Prunella, Sir Freddy)**
Placard which reads: NEVER TOO LATE TO BE HEALTHY **(Lord Brockhurst)**

Personal: **President:** dark glasses, cigar, military medals
Percy: dark glasses
Lady Brockhurst: whistle

SCENE 3

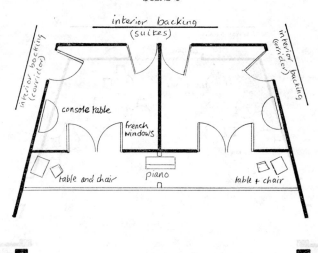

On stage: Piano which forms the parapet separating the two balconies
THE BROCKHURST SUITE (R)
On offstage wall: console table with mirror above it. *On table:* framed
photograph of Tony, telephone
On balcony: small wrought-iron table and chair

THE VAN HUSEN SUITE (L)
On offstage wall: console table with mirror above it. *On table:* framed
photograph of Maisie, telephone
On balcony: small wrought-iron table and chair

Off stage: Vase of flowers **(Solange)**
Tray. *On it:* ice-bucket with bottle of champagne, two glasses **(Raoul)**

Personal: **Bobby:** white silk scarf with monogram R

SCENE 4

On stage: As SCENE 3 except: an extra chair is set on each balcony

Off stage: Breakfast tray containing coffee for two, table cloth **(Raoul)**
Breakfast tray containing coffee for two, table cloth **(Solange)**

ACT II

SCENE 1

On stage: Nil

SCENE 2

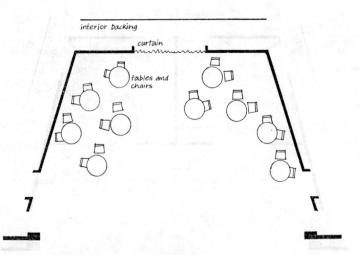

On stage: Several tables with chairs. *On tables:* glasses, ice-bucket containing bottle of champagne, etc.
Collapsible table UL (for "President")

Off stage: Broken bottle of champagne, table wreckage and debris

Personal: **Hortense:** mask
Percy: beard
Lady Brockhurst: whistle

SCENE 3

On stage: Nil

SCENE 4

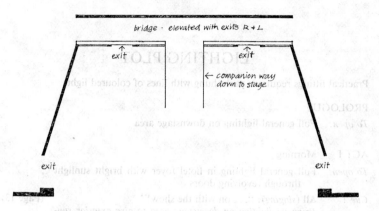

On stage: Bridge with rail
              Companionway with rail
              Bunting adorning the yacht
              Several wicker chairs along deck-side

Off stage: Scroll **(President)**

Personal: **Mme Dubonnet:** cigarette in short holder

LIGHTING PLOT

Practical fittings required: yacht hung with lines of coloured lights

PROLOGUE

To open: Full general lighting on downstage area

ACT I   Morning

To open: Full general lighting in hotel foyer with bright sunlight through revolving doors

Cue 1	**All** (*singing*): ". . . on with the show!" *Bring up lighting on downstage area to give exterior sun-light effect*	(Page 13)
Cue 2	**Percy:** "Kiki . . .!" As the music comes up to full *Lights fade to Black-out*	(Page 20)
Cue 3	As SCENE 3 opens *Evening light effect on the two balconies with artificial light-ing in suites*	(Page 20)
Cue 4	**Maisie** (*off*): "Oh . . . Bobby." *Lights fade to Black-out*	(Page 28)
Cue 5	As SCENE 4 opens *Effect of bright morning sunshine on balconies*	(Page 28)

ACT II   Night

To open: Artificial lights from inside the Café

Cue 6	As SCENE 2 opens *Bring up artificial interior lighting to full*	(Page 40)
Cue 7	As the front cloth comes in *Bring up lighting on downstage area*	(Page 44)
Cue 8	**Hannah** and **Sir Freddy** exit L *Lights fade to Black-out*	(Page 47)
Cue 9	As SCENE 4 opens *Lights up on yacht and coloured practicals on*	(Page 47)
Cue 10	As drum roll sounds *Spot comes up on the bridge and then follows* **Mme Dubonnet**	(Page 50)
Cue 11	As **Mme Dubonnet** reaches the stage *Fade spot*	(Page 50)

EFFECTS PLOT

ACT I

Cue 1	As SCENE 1 opens *Telephone rings*	(Page 3)
Cue 2	At the end of "No Harm Done" *Telephone rings in the* **Brockhurst** *suite*	(Page 24)
Cue 3	**Polly**: "I suppose it is . . ." *Telephone rings in the* **van Husen** *suite*	(Page 25)

ACT II

Cue 4	As **Lady Brockhurst**'s group perform a Swedish drill *Loud report followed by a cloud of smoke envelopping the* "**President**'s" *table and* **Lady Brockhurst**	(Page 42)

MADE AND PRINTED IN GREAT BRITAIN BY
LATIMER TREND & COMPANY LTD PLYMOUTH

MADE IN ENGLAND